Manifestations of trauma in the post-2000 Zimbabwean Literature:

An Analysis of Tendai Mwanaka's 'Notes from a Modern Chimurenga' and Christopher's Kudyahakudadirwe's 'The Big Noise and other Noises'.

NYARAI MARIA KANYEMBA

Mwanaka Media and Publishing Pvt Ltd,
Chitungwiza Zimbabwe
*
Creativity, Wisdom and Beauty

Publisher: *Mmap*
Mwanaka Media and Publishing Pvt Ltd
24 Svosve Road, Zengeza 1
Chitungwiza Zimbabwe
mwanaka@yahoo.com
mwanaka13@gmail.com
www.africanbookscollective.com/publishers/mwanaka-media-and-publishing
https://facebook.com/MwanakaMediaAndPublishing/

Distributed in and outside N. America by African Books Collective
orders@africanbookscollective.com
www.africanbookscollective.com

ISBN: 978-1-77934-083-2
EAN: 9781779340832

© Nyarai Maria Kanyemba 2024

All rights reserved.
No part of this book may be reproduced or transmitted in any form or by any means, mechanical or electronic, including photocopying and recording, or be stored in any information storage or retrieval system, without written permission from the publisher

DISCLAIMER
All views expressed in this publication are those of the author and do not necessarily reflect the views of *Mmap*.

Supervisor: Mr. E. Manotoma

A Research Project submitted to the Zimbabwe Open University in partial fulfilment of the requirements for the Bachelor of Arts degree in English and Communication Studies.

Marondera, Zimbabwe

Year: May 2023

DEDICATION

I dedicate this academic growth to my late daughter, Angela Violet Dapi. Although no longer with us in this realm, she will always be in my heart, because in there she is still alive and she is the reason why I embarked on this academic journey.

ACKNOWLEDGEMENTS

The success of this project has been made possible through valuable support of a number of individuals. First and foremost, I would like to thank the Almighty God, for his grace that sustained me throughout the years of my study. Secondly, I would like to appreciate my Program Coordinator, Doctor Sarah Yeukai Matanga, for her sterling and unwavering mentorship throughout the years of my study, she tirelessly steered me up and even encouraged me when I felt I could not continue because I had lost my daughter to a point where I felt my academic prowess weakening. I am also indebted to my project supervisor, Mr Enias Manotoma, for his professional guidance throughout the duration of my project. Special thanks go to my sister Fungai Catherine Mudyiwa who continuously supported me with internet services; I wouldn't have reached this point without her support. Lastly, to my husband, Ido and our two boys, Tatenda and Takunda, thank you for your love, support and understanding; for giving me space and time to accomplish this project.

Table of Contents

Dedication

Acknowledgement

CHAPTER ONE

BACKGROUND AND INTRODUCTION

1.0 Introduction

1.1 Background of Study

1.2 Statement of the Problem

1.3 Objectives

1.4 Research Questions

1.5 Significance of the Study

1.6 Research Methodology

1.7 Theoretical Framework

1.8 Delimitation

1.9 Limitations

1.10 Definition of Terms

1.11 Summary

CHAPTER TWO

LITERATURE REVIEW

2.0 Introduction

2.1 Unpacking Trauma Narratives

2.2 Trauma and the Post-2000 Era in Zimbabwe

2.3 Literary Representations of Trauma

2.4 Psychoanalysis and Zimbabwe post 2000 Era

2.5 Zimbabwean Traditional and Cultural beliefs on Trauma

2.6 Feminism and Trauma

2.7 Summary

CHAPTER THREE

THE CENTRE CANNOT HOLD: PARANOIC DISPLACEMENT IN MWANAKA'S NOTES FROM A MODERN CHIMURENGA

3.0 Introduction

3.1 About the Author

3.2 Historical Background

3.3 Post Modernism and other Narratives Techniques

3.4 National Insanities: Intertextual Trauma

3.5 Representation of Trauma in Creative Art

3.7 Female Victimhood and Trauma

3.8 Summary

CHAPTER FOUR

MERE ANARCHY IS LOOSENED UPON THE WORLD: THE TRAUMATIC CHAOS IN KUDYAHAKUDADIRWE'S THE BIG NOISE AND OTHER NOISES

4.0 Introduction

4.1 About the Author

4.2 Historical Background

4.3 Post2000 Features

4.4 Effects of Migration

4.5 Homosexuality

4.6 Beyond the Post-Independence Era

4.7 Summary

CHAPTER FIVE

SUMMARY, FINDINGS, CONCLUSION AND RECOMMENDATIONS

5.0 Introduction

5.1 Summary and Findings

5.2 Conclusion

5.3 Recommendations

References

Abstract

This study critically explored the depictions of trauma by two Zimbabwean authors in their post-2000 literature. The main focus was based on their reflection of trauma as either an individual state of being or as symptomatic of the socio-political and socio-economic conditions in the country. The study has adopted insights from an existential psychoanalytic framework in the literary analysis of the texts, in-order to come up with an innovative dimension to the study of this phenomena. The literary texts that the study critiqued are Christopher Kudyahakudadirwe's 'The Big Noise and other noises' and Tendai R. Mwanaka's 'Notes from a Modern Chimurenga". The study has significantly exposed how the two authors perceive and define the phenomenon in relation with the people and their environment. The investigation has revealed that trauma is intricately linked to the question of identity. This has been evidenced by its manifestations on the characters in the stories whose ontological position would have been compromised. The textual analysis of the two texts was done using the Psychoanalysis theory, the Existentialism theory and other attendant Psychosocial approaches as well as the Postmodernism and Precarity theories. The major objectives were to establish the depiction of trauma in the selected texts, to determine the extent of historical and socio-cultural factors that influence Mwanaka's and Kudyahakudadirwe's conceptualisation of trauma and to assess the impact of post-2000 Zimbabwean literature in addressing trauma. The study concluded that the texts under study provided identity formation whereby the reader is exposed to the knowledge and appreciation of the authors' experiences in the prevailing environment. The study therefore, recommends that there be literary criticism that examines how Zimbabwean fiction represents the psychological healing

CHAPTER 1

BACKGROUND AND INTRODUCTION

1.0　Introduction

This study explored how the wounded heart of a Zimbabwean as a result of emotional trauma is represented by Zimbabwean selected post-2000 literary texts edited and authored by Zimbabwean individual writers in their personal view of what has been termed as "The Zimbabwean crisis". The focus of this study is based on the reflection of trauma, as presented by selected Zimbabwean literary texts set or published after the year 2000, a period whereby the country has been in a political and economic turmoil. This is a presentation of trauma either as an individual state of being or as a symptomatic of socio-political and economic situation in the country. The selected literary texts explored are Christopher Kudyahakudadirwe's 'The Big Noise and other noises' (2018) and Tendai, R. Mwanaka's 'Notes from a Modern Chimurenga'(2020).These selected two texts afforded the opportunity to investigate the exposure of trauma as mirrored by the authors when the characters' sense of ontological security is compromised in one way or another.

1.1 Background of the Study

The selected texts in this study capture all the known events and incidents that occurred in the post 2000 Zimbabwean era crisis hence the shaping of the authors' themes in their literary texts as Okolo (2007:100) would point out, literature's "purpose is to analyse society on its terms, to present a fictional world that is a life like representation of the real world". Therefore, trauma in this context is a motif being presented either at an individual level or at a social level. The twenty - five plus stories in Notes from a Modern Chimurenga and short stories from The Big Noise and other Noises fictionally complement one another as they are all written as a reflection of Zimbabweans who are either individually or collectively wrestling with their struggles to find some ground of healing and peace.

Veit-Wild (2006:2) states that, "within the field of scholarship on African literature, the theme of madness and its relationship to writing has been little explored, and if at all, only in articles on individual works by certain writers". According to Veit-Wild, the political situation in Africa is characterised by monstrosities, absurdities and gross aberration that it demands a literary response reflecting the innermost madness of this very situation and the structures ruling it. It is within this scope of mind that the researcher, narrows down Veit-Wild's broad spectrum of African view of 'madness' to one of the discourses of madness; trauma a phenomenon that characterises Zimbabwean post-2000 literature.

According to Sachikonye (2003), between year 1999 and 2000 the Zimbabwean government initiated a violence characterised land reform program which accentuated tension and conflict among the Zimbabweans. The land reform program has combined with other factors that include; drought, the AIDS pandemic, economic instability, ineffective economic policies, poor public services and poor health delivery system to induce some form of trauma to the majority of Zimbabweans. Paula (2016) is espoused to the same notion as he states that the political situation in Zimbabwe is getting worse, as evidenced by the mass protests, job stay aways, corruption, bond notes and lack of socio-political and economic development amongst many other things being experienced in Zimbabwe.

1.2 Statement of the problem

The reading of the texts; 'Notes from a Modern Chimurenga' and 'The Big Noise and other noises may be viewed as descriptive narratives of the post-2000 events but very few works link the narratives with the wounds that the Zimbabweans have as a result of traumatic experiences in the post-Zimbabwean era.

1.3 Objectives

The study was carried out under the following objectives:-

- To establish the depiction of trauma in the selected texts
- To determine the extent of historical and socio-cultural factors that influence Mwanaka's and Kudyahakudadirwe's conceptualisation of trauma.
- To assess the impact of post-2000 Zimbabwean literature in addressing trauma.

1.4 Research Questions

- How do selected texts define and depict trauma?
- What is the effect of post-2000 Zimbabwean literature on the subject of trauma?
- How can literary texts be used in addressing trauma?

1.5 Significance of the study

The post-colonial Zimbabwean literature is predominantly characterised by the socio–economic and socio-political struggles that the authors' protagonists experience which resultantly impacted negatively on their sense of identity and an ambiguous state of being. Be that as it may, not much literary criticism exists on the effects of these struggles which include mental issues, thus, constituting a scholarly vacuum.

This study also helped to understand how trauma is represented in Zimbabwean literature through themes of cultural alienation which results in otherness, exile and marginalisation as a state of being that the protagonists suffer.

1.6 Research Methodology

As a literary research, the study was conducted using a qualitative research methodology based on textual analysis of the selected texts whereby meaning of the text was perceived through the lenses of the characters, their situation and environment. The study explored in-depth traumatic issues from two literature texts written by Zimbabwean writers. The texts were then analysed using thematic analysis method to generate emerging themes.

1.7 Theoretical framework

This study was undertaken based on theories that inform both literature and social psychology. From a literary point of view, theories such as, Psychoanalysis, Postmodernism, Precarity and Existentialism were methods used to analyse the texts. From a Social Psychological perspective, Psychosocial approach was used to inform the study. The theories that inform literature basically focus on the environment in which the literary works were written whilst those from a Social Psychology focus on the influence of people on one another and this combination gives a basis of an individual's identity formation.

1.8 Delimitation

By focusing on the post-2000 Zimbabwean crisis, this research highlighted the presentation and depiction of trauma from two post-2000 Zimbabwean literature; Tendai R. Mwanaka's 'Notes from a Modern Chimurenga' (2020) and Christopher Kudyahakudadirwe's 'The Big Noise and other noises' (2018). The research showed how the selected short stories from the two authors interrogate the ontological status of the protagonists thereby circumventing the notion of trauma in post-2000 Zimbabwean literature.

1.9 Limitations

The smooth progress of the research was hindered by a number of challenges that included the economic crisis that is bedevilling the country, the intermittent availability of communication networks and the power outages that are being experienced in almost every part of the country. The researcher worked under pressure as the time frame given to submit the research was very short. Be that as it may the researcher worked tirelessly against these odds to write and submit the project well in time.

1.10 Definition of Terms

Trauma - an emotional response to a terrible event.

Post-2000 Zimbabwean Literature - Zimbabwean Literary texts set or published after year 2000.

Literature - Any collection of written work.

Representation- State of serving a mission

Socio-economic - a combination of social and economic factors.

Socio-political - a combination of social and political factors

Gukurahundi -A genocide which arose in Zimbabwe in 1982

Chimurenga - Shona word which means a struggle or a fight.

1.11 Summary

This chapter has provided the introduction and background to the study, outlining the key research questions as well as giving a clear indication and justification of the research. It has also given the definition of trauma and other relevant terms in relation with the study. In addition, the chapter has stated the problem as well as supplied the theoretical framework underpinning the study. The chapter has also given the delimitation and limitations to the study as well outlining the organisation of the study through a delineation of various chapters. The next chapter will provide an overview of scholarly literature and debates that relate to the theme of trauma.

CHAPTER TWO

LITERATURE REVIEW

2.0 Introduction

In this chapter, the researcher provides an extensive review of literature that gives a fundamental background to the study of the theme of trauma in the post-2000 Zimbabwean literary context. The main objective is to have the research placed in the larger bodies of relevant scholarship and demonstrate how this study is going to carry forward the existing academic debates on this particular theme. The researcher begins by giving a background and history of trauma narratives as a foundation to the study, outlining how the writers on this subject have dealt with this phenomenon in their texts.

This chapter again gives a general review of the existing critical scholarship on trauma in African literature as well as on the development of literary criticism on the subject within Zimbabwe. This synopsis is going to help the researcher to find out how the selected

Zimbabwean post-2000 writers deal with the theme of trauma and this will take cognizance of traditional and cultural beliefs based on a major ethnic group; that is, the Shona culture. The literature review that will be done will help to situate the interface of trauma and art. The study will not end if the question of gender is not considered in relation to the theme of trauma, therefore the chapter will examine how the issue of gender is dealt with in the literary texts that depict the theme of trauma. Lastly, the chapter will end by looking at how the selected Zimbabwean post-2000 writers employ literary techniques and styles in both form and language of their texts to present the theme of trauma.

2.1 Unpacking trauma narratives

As trauma is a state of an ill mental state, Foucault (1961)'s discourse suggests that human beings institutionalize or confine mental instability because it represents a social disorder, that is something to be ashamed of, feared or a malfunction of a social system. According to Foucault's school of thought, mental instability is a social construct rather than a biological evil. This means that trauma is a condition that comes when the normal social system is violated thereby disrupting the social order as opposed to being a state that is brought about by biological effects. This fact is illustrated in the play 'She No Longer Weeps' by Dangarembga, when Martha, the main female protagonist is severely traumatized by the patriarchal system in her society which has violated the boundaries of her dreams and beliefs.

Like Foucault, Dangarembga seems to suggest here that trauma is indeed a social construct defined by the society in which it exists. The gendered language she employs implies that within a patriarchal society, men as the dominant sex, they are accountable to the social and cultural space in which trauma and its effects are exhibited. Martha in 'She No Longer Weeps' represents a visible mental disorder which Foucault's discourse suggests that there is a reason or logic to the disorder. This therefore means that Martha suffers trauma due to a number of reasons which include rejection amongst many other reasons that are caused by a patriarchal system.

According to Hartmann (Nd), trauma narratives are simply connecting the writers and their readers, whereby the writers are simply giving testimonials of present or past painful experiences and the readers are decoding these painful experiences and messages that are being sent to them, thus the traumatic experiences being expressed by the writers are also felt by the readers. Readers are exposed to various triggers of trauma which are presented at various historical dispensations. Kanengoni (1997)'s Echoing Silence presents how the novel's main protagonist Munashe Mungate is traumatized by the Zimbabwean Liberation war and its aftermaths thereby exposing the readers to the traumatic effects of both the colonial era and the post- independence era in Zimbabwe.

Muchemwa et al (2014:8) citing Hove, cited by Veit-Wild describes the function of a writer as "bleeding, mourning and despairing with the voiceless, the powerless and the victims of both power and circumstance". This means that the trauma narratives do reflect a growing awareness of the effect's catastrophe and oppression of an individual's psyche, a state of mind that has been affected by the effects of periods of unprecedented social, economic and political changes, genocide and disappearing cultures amongst many other effects. The researcher will then proceed to consider how the social, cultural, economic and political structures of the post-2000 crisis in Zimbabwe may have triggered bouts of trauma to the Zimbabweans.

2.2 Trauma and the Post-2000 Era in Zimbabwe

The post-2000 Zimbabwean crisis has literally informed the post-2000 Zimbabwean literature as the texts are capturing both the developments and the turmoil that are being experienced in the country. All known developments and incidents in this particular era do form a backdrop on which all texts are based on with the writers fictionalizing the actual situation on the ground which is mainly characterized by hardships that include political crisis, land disputes, mass migration, joblessness, starvation, hyperinflation, HIV and AIDS pandemic, cholera, violation of human rights, shortcomings of the indigenization policy and socio–political impasse.

According to Hochbruck (1994), the Second Chimurenga ended through negotiations leading to the end of the colonial rule thus bringing a shift in power structure that brought about the black government.

The economic status remained predominantly white; the white minority remained the owners of key industries and the most productive land. The black bourgeoisie leadership betrayed the majority of the Zimbabweans and dismally failed to fulfill the hopes of ordinary Zimbabweans. The black leadership is purely focusing on enriching itself at the expense of its black majority counterparts. This is in Achebe's terms, "where the rain started to beat us," Achebe (1964), thus creating a historical background on the post-2000 crisis.

Fanon (1967), through his mental patients who were subjected to colonization reveals that the patients suffer considerable psychological problems induced by colonization. He goes on to say that the relationship between the colonizer and the colonized has created a "massive psyche existential complex" which means that the colonized are made conscious that they are always objects rather than subjects. This collective neurosis and mental disintegration still prevail in the post-2000 period in Zimbabwe where there is a continuation of political and mental repression that started with colonialism. The ordinary Zimbabweans have remained objects in the hands of the black leadership instead of being the subjects they hoped to be after colonial rule. At this point, the researcher goes on to give insight on the relationship that exists between literature and trauma.

2.3 Literary representations of Trauma

Felman (2003) believes that madness that the society silences is given voice by literature, when she compares madness and literature, this therefore means that trauma experiences in any society is given voice by literature. In this context it means that literature has a role to play in influencing people in the way they define and perceive mental health; and literature itself is affected by these human perceptions. Thus, literature and trauma inform each other thus creating a bond between these two.

Caruth (1995:18) asserts that there is a link that connects psychoanalysis and literature when she states: "…Freud turns to literature to describe traumatic experience it is because literature like psychoanalysis is interested in the complex relation between knowing and not knowing. And it is indeed at the specific point at which knowing and not knowing intersect that the language of literature and psychoanalytic theory of traumatic experience precisely meet". Caruth (ibid) here is implying that once one goes through a traumatic experience, they do not assimilate it, that is they do not know but it is in the telling and retelling of the traumatic experience through literature that it is actually known and felt. Rieger (1994) goes on to elaborate that victims of trauma may not want to show their traumatic states to other people within their society and literature comes in to clarify the situations and provides insight into understanding ourselves and others.

In the African context, the theme of trauma is dominant in the continent's literature as earlier mentioned in the introduction, with both female and male authors addressing the phenomenon as the writers are dealing with the traumatic experiences of various historical dispensations that include colonialism and racism. Ramadanovic (2001:2) asserts this notion when he states that "What makes literature into the privileged…. site of trauma is the fact that literature as an art form can contain and present an aspect of experience which was not experienced or processed fully. Literature in other words, because of its sensible and representational character, because of its figurative language, is a channel and a medium of transmission of trauma which does not need to be apprehended in order to be present in a text or in order to be witnessed".

Renowned African writers have explored the theme of trauma such as Achebe (1958) in 'Things Fall Apart', the protagonist Okonkwo is so much consumed by an excessive fear of failure; he ends up committing suicide leaving the villagers shocked by this abnormal act which clearly presents a state of psychological impasse on Okonkwo. Marechera (1978) 'House of Hunger', Dangarembga (1996) 'Nervous conditions, Chidora (2019 'Because Sadness is beautiful' and Chinodya (1989) 'Harvest of Thorns' are some of the literary texts that deal with trauma to some degree. In conclusion, this section has illustrated that literature does indeed serve an important role in the definition and understanding of trauma and the next section illustrates the interconnectedness of psychoanalysis and the post-2000 era.

2.4 Psychoanalysis and Zimbabwe Post-2000 era

There is a strong connection that exists between psychoanalysis and various historical dispensations in the Zimbabwean literature. According to Zhuwarara's (2001:10) observation "Zimbabwean fiction is responsive to and reflective of historical processes which affect society as a whole" This observation, suggests that history and fiction move alongside each other which means that the historical experience sheds considerable measure of light on the tone, form, content and thematic preoccupation of the fiction. It is within this framework that the post-2000 Zimbabwean literature reflects the Zimbabwean crisis in this era thus connecting history and fiction. Zimbabwe endured almost a century of colonialism, an experience that negatively impacted on the psyche and culture of its black people and this scarred psychological and cultural identity still affects the majority of them in the post –colonial era as evidenced by the literature of this period.

Fanon (1967b) argues that only when the socio–economic structures in African nations are changed to materially empower the black people can their neurosis be healed. This simply means that, in the Zimbabwean context trauma at an individual level must be considered in relation to the larger socio-historical forces at play in the post-2000 era and if remedial action is taken to empower the ordinary Zimbabwean will heal the nation. The post-2000 literary texts are merely giving testimonies of the Zimbabwean post-2000 political and cultural contexts to the readers exposing the creativity of the human mind in exposing the traumatic experiences at hand.

2.5 Zimbabwean Traditional and Cultural Beliefs on Trauma

In Zimbabwe, trauma manifests itself differently in different cultures with a particular culture specifying its own symptoms with main ethnic groups identifying the symptoms of the phenomenon as madness, a broad umbrella term for various discourses of mental illness. Chavhunduka (1994:81 - 82) cited by Veit–Wild (2006) gives a varying cause of manifestations as "Firstly, there are natural factors such as brain damage, poor brain development, and incorrect use of medicines. In the second group of factors responsible for mental illness are psychological factors such as worry, strain, and tension. Related to the second group of factors are the various social agencies that cause illness, such as ancestor spirits, angry spirits, witches, alien spirits and sorcerers". In Zimbabwe it is perceived that mental challenges are dominantly caused by factors in the third group.

In Kanengoni's 'Echoing Silences' (1997), Munashe, the main protagonist who ruthlessly kills a woman with a baby on her back, is haunted by the traumatic memory of the war right up to the end of his life. Taking it from a cultural point of view, it may be perceived that Munashe is being haunted by the spirit of 'ngozi' (avenging spirits), when in actual fact it is his mind which is affected by the traumatic events that took place during the liberation war. The researcher then proceeded to look at how the authors of the post-2000 narratives employ literary techniques as they present the theme of trauma.

2.6 Feminism and Trauma

Various scholars have come up with a variety of definitions of feminism, and all of them point out to the effect that it is a set of ideologies whose aim is to establish and define socio-political, economic and personal equality of both sexes. Traditionally feminist advocacy is biased on women's rights, their social standing as well as their general living experiences, claiming their position as equals not as subordinate members of a society. (Crawford 2006). Feminism theory believes that women are subjugated to various forms of patriarchal repression hence the need to fight against all forms of sexism and patriarchy. Achifusi (1987:40) gives a very relevant definition of feminism to this study as "…politics directed at changing existing power relations between men and women in society. The power relations structure of all areas of life, the family, education and welfare, the worlds of work and politics, culture and leisure. They determine who does what, for whom, what we are and what we might become".

The philosophy of feminism has been used to study literature as early as the Victorian age whereby critical analysis of female authored texts as well as female protagonists help in investigating the extent at which societal structures contribute to women's traumatic moments. For example, the traumatic experience that Neria goes through after her husband dies in Dangarembga's film Neria. As much as the philosophy of feminism fights for the eradication of sexist domination for the positive transformation of a woman, there are other factors that include racial and socio-economic forces that may also lead women to experience trauma.

According to Veit-Wild (2006:127), the psychiatric discourse on African women has been of "rampant sexuality, hysteria and unruliness" as the women are labeled "wandering wombs, walking vaginas, and menopausal witches". This means that African women's identities are so much compromised and they are culturally alienated from their society as they are perceived as beings of lesser value thereby compromising their ontological state of being. According to Shelton (2004:351) when a woman's sense of self is compromised, she may resort to bizarre acts in a bid to escape "existential disease of belonging nowhere, of being deprived of identity". This interconnectedness of women's identity and trauma is explored in Dangarembga's text 'She No Longer Weeps' when Martha kills her husband as well as in Vera's 'Butterfly Burning' when Phephelaphi aborts her unborn baby and commits suicide. In the next section the researcher will discuss how the traditional and cultural beliefs of the Zimbabwean society interlink with mental health.

2.8 Summary

This chapter has given an elaborated review of literature that is relevant to the representations of trauma in post-2000 Zimbabwean literature. It has provided the necessary background knowledge and different perceptions on the phenomenon that will help in the critical analysis of the different authors' conceptualization of trauma in the post-2000 Zimbabwean context as revealed in their literary texts. The next chapter will fully explore the theme of trauma by critiquing Mwanaka's conceptualization of trauma in 'Notes from a Modern Chimurenga' where a collection of short stories is written from the perception of an ordinary Zimbabwean in the post-2000 era.

CHAPTER 3

THE CENTER CANNOT HOLD: PARANOIAC DISPLACEMENT IN MWANAKA'S NOTES FROM A MODERN CHIMURENGA (2020)

3.0 Introduction

The previous chapter provided a literature review that is relevant to this study on the representations of trauma in the post-2000 Zimbabwean literature. In this chapter, the researcher explored the issues such as the background of trauma. The researcher's critical literary analysis in this chapter was based on how Mwanaka (2020) handles the theme of trauma in 'Notes from a Modern Chimurenga'. Mwanaka's twenty-five plus stories are written from an individual struggle, wrestling with their situation and trying to find some form of healing from various traumatic experiences protagonists. Mwanaka does not only depict the psychosis that the protagonists suffer, but also explores manifestations of trauma in the Zimbabwean landscape. In this chapter the researcher presented how this text is considered to be having characteristics of a psychotic text which are exposed through Mwanaka's adoption of postmodernist techniques in his narratives.

3.1 About the Author

Tendayi. R. Mwanaka is a multi-disciplinary artist who hails from the dormitory town of Chitungwiza in Zimbabwe. His oeuvre of works touches on non-fictions, essays, poetry, plays, fictions, music, sound art, photography, drawings, paintings, video collage, mixed media, inter genres and interdisciplines. Mwanaka's works has appeared in more than 400 literary journals in several countries that include the UK, USA, France, Spain and other African countries. His works have been reviewed in more than 20 places that include the National newspapers of different countries. He has written 24 books and has published and edited 90 books under his Mwanaka Media and Publishing Company.

3.2 Historical Background

Notes from a Modern Chimurenga is an extensive collection of Zimbabwe's political struggle short stories covering the modern Chimurenga period from the formation of tribal trust lands, the liberation wars, the Gukurahundi massacres, the late 1990s democratic struggles pitting ZANU PF against the MDC, the individual struggle within this democratic struggle, the resultant migration and exilitic stories, the mismanagement of the country, the beatings and killings and the continuing democratic struggles. The stories are written from the perspective of the common on the streets; not from an elite's perspective which therefore means that the stories are relatable to the struggle that is being faced by the ordinary person in Zimbabwe.

3.3 Post-modernism and other Narrative Techniques

The story Hero of Zeros is based on Joseph the main protagonist whose pay slip has reached the 1 000 000 mark and he has to withdraw lots and lots of bills from the bank to procure the basic necessities. This scenario reminds him of the story of the Tokoloshi that puked money that he has heard as a young boy. Joseph likens the story with his position, in as much as he cannot do anything about the zeroes that was the same scenario that was faced by the man who owned the Tokoloshi who succumbed to the endless demands of the Tokoloshi.

In the story, 'Hero of Zeroes', Mwanaka, does not show linearity, in the plot as he subtly orchestrates the story to go backwards and forth in time from the past to the present, as it unveils the events of this particular story. This seems to be a deliberate ploy employed by the author to reflect the fragmented psyche of Joseph when his mind spirals with chaotic thoughts as he moves between reality and delusion from his world of things. It is left to the reader to make a distinction between the blurry of facts and the fiction of the Joseph's imagination.

The theme of trauma is fundamentally exposed through the narrative form of the text that is employed by Mwanaka. According to Stone (2004:12), many authors who write on the psychic theme do pose the Kofman's question concerning speaking the unspeakable, "and crucially their texts bear witness to their various attempts to manage and stretch the constraints inherent in conventional narrative forms." The title of the story; 'Hero of Zeroes' is a representation of fragmentation of form, according to

Chiridza (2015), titles provide a frame for the reading of setting and characters as well as providing clues to content and style. Therefore in this context, Mwanaka exposes the traumatic experiences of Joseph, who is a Hero for nothing.

Fragmentation of form is also evident in Mwanaka's text, when he employs radical typographical methods, for instance in the title of the story, 'Operation Murambatsvina'. The story is based on the protagonist Tyson who resides in Chitungwiza together with his family. His family together with other families is affected by the operation Murambatsvina and they are left homeless. Mwanaka distorts the conventional typography on the word 'Murambatsvina' to emphasize the level of psychological effects the operation had on its victims. Mwanaka uses different typography (italicized words) in this story and other stories to indicate the shift of the narrative voice away from the omniscient third person narrator to interior monologue as he dives into characters in the stories. Fragmentation of form is further evident in the last part of the story, 'Operation Murambatsvina' when Mwanaka gives a synopsis of the story at the end (p.134) to stress the intensity of the psychological effects of the matter.

"This aptly entitled "Operation Murambatsvina program made over 700 000 people to become homeless in Zimbabwe's cities. It later became known as "operation Zvipwanyirewega" (operation destroy it yourself), after people took it over from the government and started doing the destruction themselves of their own illegal structures. If they had waited for the government's destroyers, they would have lost possessions like furniture and kitchen utensils in the government's utterly insensitive drive. The government's drive didn't care about what was inside those structures. The graders just struck the structures and a number of people had died in this government's drive, so to be on the safe side, you had to destroy it yourself".

This therefore, gives a reality representation of events that occurred during the operation Murambatsvina.

3.4 National Insanities – Intertextual Trauma in Notes from a Modern Chimurenga

Mwanaka's literary works are based on the backdrop of societal change that has been influenced by the political situation of the era. As Ngugi (1997:19) would put it across, "Whether or not he is aware of it, his (the writer) works reflect one or more aspects of the intense economic, political, cultural and ideological struggles in his society. What he can choose is one or the other side of those forces that try to keep people down. What he cannot do is to remain neutral. Every writer is a writer in politics. The only question is what and whose politics". It is within this scope of mind that Mwanaka's Notes from a Modern Chimurenga is an exploration of the human condition in the face of socio-political and socio–economic problems without articulating possible practical solutions to them.

When Mwanaka points to trauma in relation to other texts outside of 'Notes from a Modern Chimurenga', he therefore, engages in intertextuality as a deliberate stylistic device to mirror the cultural and socio-political discourses of the times in Zimbabwe that he writes about, and which are subsumed with the larger plot. According to Wilson-Tagoe (1999), intertextuality is defined as the implicit and explicit interaction between texts, forms, genres and discourses. In this context it means the interconnection between Mwanaka's literary text and its non-literary context. Nyambi (2011:9) states that "intertextuality assumes that literary works are just a kind of texts that are congeneric to other non–literary texts and therefore their meanings can adequately infer when the literary text is analyzed in relation to these 'other texts'". The philosophy behind this concept suggests that a text does not only depend on the creativity of the author but also on the social and historical construct.

The intertextuality of 'Notes from a Modern Chimurenga' points to the existential nature of all the protagonists in the stories in relation to the world around them. Therefore, Mwanaka's discourse on trauma includes the socio-political and socio-economic insanities that bedeviled the nation in the post-2000 era, a period referred to by Sachikonye (2012:23) as one of Zimbabwe's "lost decades". This era was characterized by a steep decline in the country's economy as well as violation of human rights by the government on Non-governmental Organizations personnel and opposition leaders and activists. The female protagonist, who is the first part narrator and her counterparts in the story, 'The list' are traumatized in the hands of the Central Intelligence personnel who clearly state that "We don't do torture, we do enhanced interrogation, Madam". (p1).

Notes from a Modern Chimurenga' cannot be classified as committed literature because, although Mwanaka highlights the various traumatic experiences that the nation endures triggered by socio-political and socio-economic woes, he does not suggest any possible reforms to alleviate the phenomenon that has affected the Zimbabwean society. Despite everyone being a 'millionaire', the majority of Zimbabweans failed to secure basic necessities and it was a period when the country experienced great shortages and supermarket shelves were empty. By 2007, that economic chaos resulted in the massive migration of close to 25% of the population. (Sachikonye 2012). Families were split up due to pervasive exodus of people to the Diaspora, the neighboring countries such as South Africa and Botswana in search of economic sustenance.

In the text, the story 'Limpopo's bones', exposes the trauma that the Zimbabweans go through in their exility process. The title of the story metaphorically gives a representation of how the Zimbabweans risk their lives as they expose themselves to the dangers of the Limpopo River when they use the illegal route of having to enter South Africa through the river points.

Half the time the illegal immigrants would be robbed and physically abused by the Malaitshas (border gangsters). Some of them would even die in the process as presented by Sibusiso a former Malaitsha who is haunted by the death of a woman and her child who were torn by crocodiles while he watched. The story also exposes the traumatic experiences that the Zimbabweans go through when they eventually manage to cross the border, their living conditions are deplorable as presented by the setting of the room that Sibusiso and Chengetai share.

3.5 Representation of trauma in Creative Art

Several psychoanalytic studies have explored the connection between creativity and mental illness; mental instability, therefore, believed to sometimes enhance the level of creativity; (Saunders and Macnaughton 2005). This means that the relationship between creativity and trauma is not only linked to the cognitive domain, but to the affective one too, as reflected in mood disorders that creative people experience; a condition that is reflected on Takunda, the main protagonist in the story, 'Chitungwiza'.

Somerville (2012:191) posits that creativity itself requires "intense levels of energy, passion and daring" and in the text, Mwanaka's protagonist in the story 'Chitungwiza' appears to possess all the three aspects. Takunda is a young man who seems to be in a traumatic situation as his neighbors think he is lazy and is fond of sleeping, but he doesn't see the laziness in him but the laziness in the councilors who are not doing their jobs as evidenced by continuous bursts of sewer pipes. His creativity, however, has made him a prominent artist in the text, whose intense levels of energy and passion have made him stand up against all odds in the fight against inhumanity in his society.

Saunders and Macnaughton (2005:203) state that "the great artist has a greater capacity to tap into the unconscious fantasy than ordinary mortals have, which accounts, in part, for the power of great art. Everybody fantasizes, although this capacity, as we know, can be unhealthily inhibited, but when fantasies take over the mind in an over powerful, over luxuriant way, then this leads to neurosis, or psychosis." This is exactly what happens to Takunda at some point, "It has been on and off for a year now. One week it is bursting and flowing off – and after some couple of weeks, the lazy council guys will stench off the flow. It would hold for a week, and then it would burst off and start flowing again. To Takunda it has created an outlet for his creative mind." (p.108). This therefore means that Takunda feels he can encompass the whole scenario in the art form.

3.6 Female Victimhood and 'Trauma'

Mwanaka's anthology deliberately depicts issues that affect women's ontological state of position during the post-2000 crisis because it is assumed that women suffer the most during moments of crisis but their sufferings are often ignored and their voices are even silenced in artistic productions. However, Mwanaka's anthology has been able to depict the disintegration of families resulting in great physical and emotional pain to all, especially women. The socio–economic and socio–political struggles in the post-2000 era in Zimbabwe have affected women in a unique and often uncelebrated ways; (Nyambi 2014). Most of the stories are better understood through Butler's notion of 'Precarity;' (Butler 2009). She states that 'precarity' designates politically induced conditions in which some sections of populations are vulnerable as they fail to get social and economic support systems and are exposed to violence, injury and even death. Most of the female characters in Mwanaka's 'Notes from a Modern Chimurenga' are in situations which Butler refers to as "heightened risk of disease, poverty, starvation, displacement, and of exposure to violence without protection" (2009:ii)

The state of desperation on all the female protagonists in the stories is synonymous with what Butler (2009) refers to as the social safety nets that have been torn asunder, there by leaving the family unit vulnerable. In the story 'Karidza', Mai Karidza is traumatized as she witnesses her husband being brutally murdered by ZANU PF party activists, their crime is being activists of the opposition party. She is also severely assaulted; this leaves Mai Karidza in a traumatic situation; a widow who will now have to continue facing the political violence and the socio-economic hardships of the post–2000 crisis on her own, her family unit has been disbanded, her husband who was her only family has been brutally taken away from her and they did not have any child from their marriage.

In the story 'Chitungwiza', Mwanaka highlights how Kristina suffers as a woman because she has to fend for her children on her own. She dropped out of school in the first year of her secondary education because she had been impregnated. She got pregnant again for the second, third and fourth time with different men. She stayed briefly in a marriage but it did not last as the man ran off to South Africa and she is left with four children to take care of. Although Kristina had settled into a career as a street hawker, she does not get enough to take care of the basic needs of her children. This situation is made worse when she is jailed together with Takunda, her children are left with no one look after them.

The same story explores the impact of HIV and AIDS on women in relation to the Zimbabwean politically induced socio–economic precarity of the post-2000 period which allows us to explore HIV and AIDS as a 'discursive formation'. The story participates in a discourse on HIV and AIDS and sexual morality. The patriarchal nature of the Zimbabwean community does not uphold certain moral norms associated with sexuality. Matibenga (2007) has made an observation that the HIV and AIDS pandemic in Zimbabwe increased the challenges faced by women. Madam Kunofiwa is in a precarious economic situation in Zimbabwe as she is exposed to the HIV virus because she uses her body to entice different men at different levels and besides being exposed to the HIV virus, she has five children with different men.

Mwanaka employs toponymy and satire in the story 'Notes from Mai Mujuru's breast' to present a corruption scenario in the Marange diamond fields. As a woman and a mother, people expect her to use her feminine qualities to ensure that ordinary people are provided for, Mwanaka does not bind the 'breast' symbol to a particular or discursive meaning, he creates what Langer (1979:238) calls "ambivalence of meaning, which allows greater freedom for literary imagination" concerning the quality of diamonds and lack of accessibility to the diamond fields. The section named 'Zamu ra Mai Mujuru' (Mrs.Mujuru's breast) has the most expensive diamonds and are in the highly protected area.

In this story Mwanaka uses explicit sexual imagery of a woman, to show how a woman could be a source of misery and trauma. "If you were to lick a bit of that breast, you would go home smiling...." (p.141). The use of the word 'lick' evokes a sexual act as the narrator likens the mounds of earth that contain the precious mineral with that of Joyce Mujuru's actual breasts. The urge to access the diamond is equated to making love to Mai Mujuru as the boys talk of their desire "to taste Mai Mujuru's huge mounds?" (breasts)(p.141). Mwanaka uses the imagery of a woman to highlight the callousness of the government as the narrator presents how people were traumatized by the military and in fact some were even killed (p.141). This fictional account is supported by Sachikonye (2011) who estimates that up to 20 000 people were killed in 2008 as the state sought to exert control over diamond mining.

3.7 Summary

In this chapter, the main aim was to explore Mwanaka's varied depictions of trauma in 'Notes from a Modern Chimurenga'. It is evident from the above discussion that Mwanaka's allusions to cultural, political and socio-economic discourses are indicative of both national and individual trauma of the times in Zimbabwe. The literary analysis has shown that indeed there is a connection between creativity and trauma as evidenced by the protagonist in the text 'Takunda;' creativity is literally connected to his sense of ontology. This chapter has also shown that in 'Notes from a Modern Chimurenga', Mwanaka takes cognizance of the Zimbabwean cultural beliefs in relation with trauma. Lastly; the literary analysis has shown how Mwanaka has mirrored the image of women in the face of trauma phenomenon. In the next chapter the researcher examined how Kudyahakudadirwe depicts trauma in his text 'The big Noise and other noises'

CHAPTER 4

"MERE ANARCHY IS LOOSED UPON THE WORLD": THE TRAUMATIC CHAOS IN KUDYAHAKUDADIRWE'S THE BIG NOISE AND OTHER NOISES.

4.0 Introduction

The previous chapter explored how Mwanaka perceives trauma based on socio-political and cultural environment in the post-2000 era. This particular chapter investigates how Kudyahakudadirwe depicts the phenomenon based on the chaotic crisis in the post 2000 era and beyond the era in; 'The Big Noise and Other Noises' (2018). The text traces the journeys of several protagonists in the short stories as they struggle to deal with the cultural and psychological trauma of living in a shattered Zimbabwe where everything has just gone wrong and things are not working as they should be.

4.1 About the Author

Christopher Kudyahakudadirwe is a Zimbabwean freelance writer, poet and teacher living and working in

South Africa. His first poems appeared in a magazine called Tsotso which was published by the Budding Writers Association of Zimbabwe in the early 90s. His poems have been published in several anthologies that include Creative Writing Poetry Anthology and Zimbolicious Poetry Anthology. He is currently running a poetry blog called www.kudyahakudadirwe.wordpress.com where he publishes his own poems.

4.2 Historical Background of the text

The Big Noise and other noises (2018) is a collection of short stories that are written from an ordinary Zimbabwean's perception. The stories are on a chaotic situation in the post-independent Zimbabwean era where a big frightening noise of approaching caterpillars sent by government to build a new dam is heard and other conflicting noises are heard as the same government has again sent the caterpillars to destroy the people's homes. There are several noises to be heard as Zimbabwe is in a chaotic situation as the then, 93 year old president is forced to announce his resignation amid the noises of confusion as graduates are jobless and people are fleeing the country to other countries to become political as well as economic refugees.

4.3 Post-2000 Features

This section of the analysis focuses on Kudyahakudadirwes's depiction of trauma trope in response to the political, social, and economic crisis in the post-2000 Zimbabwean era. It is this psychic wound of an ordinary Zimbabwean that has been caused by the post-independence colonialism that Kudyahakudadirwe is concerned about in his text; 'The Big Noise and other noises'. Chapter three of this study, extensively dealt with the post-2000 economic crisis that ravaged the country and that negatively affected the quality of the livelihoods of the majority of Zimbabweans. The chapter extensively discussed how this economic meltdown referred to by Sachikonye (2012) as a lost decade caused national economic insanities. Kudyahakudadirwe highlights some of the results of the economic downside of the era such as the increased migrations of people to the Diaspora to become economic and political refugees and jobless graduates.

In the story; 'Deformed Dreams', Kudyahakudadirwe exposes the economic trauma experienced by an unnamed young protagonist who has attained his degree but has failed to get a job to sustain himself. The narrator is sympathizing with the traumatic situation that this young protagonist is going through as he has failed to secure even menial jobs. Chronicling the job-hunting event in the days of the week, from Monday to Friday, not even a single day has brought joy to this young graduate. The tone of the sympathizing narrator exposes the emptiness of the Zimbabwean government's rhetoric about the empowerment of Zimbabweans through economic development as evidenced on (p.9) when the narrator states that the unnamed graduate has voted for the current government believing that the economy would be on the mend birthing jobs as per its empty promises.

In this story, Kudyahakudadirwe is exposing the emotional turmoil that is experienced by the young Zimbabwean graduates whose hopes are shattered by the prevailing economic crisis. Be that as it may, the psychological impact of the post-2000 crisis in Zimbabwe has led to some people adopting various coping mechanisms. For example, the narrator refers

Friday as the *'Faraiday'* (day to be happy) where people would celebrate it in many ways to drown their problems (p.94). These people are forced by their precarious situations to enter into what Agamben (2000) refers to as 'the zone of none being'. This zone of non-being creates a state of madness which helps the people to escape their unavoidable challenges. Unfortunately, the social support system cannot help either as it can only watch and sympathize as presented by the narrator, this therefore means that it is a vicious social traumatic cycle affecting everyone in the society. For instance, the widowed mother of this unnamed graduate "had literally closed her livestock pens….;" (p.92), in the hope that this graduate will have a future, so in this case it is the politically induced trauma that births the social trauma and this cycle keeps on revolving within a given society. In this context, the trauma cycle revolves around the graduate, his mother and the people around him who are represented by the sympathizing narrator. This therefore, means that society as a whole can no longer uphold its existential security. The Thursday that the university graduates play soccer in First Street in their graduation regalia; Kudyahakudadirwe satirically points to a direct attack on the government of Zimbabwe that has abdicated its social and economic responsibility in taking care of its people. This means that Kudyahakudadirwe has ironically rendered the Zimbabwean education useless.

The story; 'Between a Rock and a Hard Place', is an allegory or an allusion to the Zimbabwean chaotic situation, the story exposes the social decadence in hierarchical levels of the Zimbabwean society. Kudyahakudadirwe uses the story to expose themes of betrayal, promiscuity and thievery which have traumatic damaging effects on social relations. Karasa the main protagonist in the story realizes that his family has lost one of their oxen that they use to plough. After a long search, he ends up at the chief's homestead where his ox had been last seen, and he gets entangled in the feasting and partying that is taking place at the homestead, little does he know that the chunks of meat that people are eating are being taken from his lost ox. The story whose setting is on a rural landscape metaphorically highlights the Marxism hierarchical trauma that takes place there, whereby the upper class is capitalizing through the exploitation of the lower class. The story suggests that the desperate and the poor are victims of the larger powerful sources.

The story clearly exposes the inherent opportunism of the ruling elite in Zimbabwe who take care of their interests at the expense of the poor thereby creating a widening gap between the poor and the rich. This is substantiated by Fanon (1963:138) when he states that "There exists inside the new regime, however, an inequality in the acquisition of wealth and in monopolization. Some have a double source of income and demonstrate that they are specialized in opportunism. Privileges multiply and corruption triumphs, while morality declines. Today the vultures are too numerous and too voracious in proportion to the lean spoils of the national wealth. The party, a true instrument of power in the hands of the bourgeoisie, reinforces the machine, and ensures that the people are hemmed in and immobilized. The party helps the government to hold the people down." Kudyahakudadirwe hints on the social trauma that takes place when the ruling party is at the center of denying people better livelihoods through its unjust system of corruptly acquiring wealth at the expense of the ordinary Zimbabwean. The chief who is a representation of the ruling class does not respect his social status he slaughters an ox that does not belong to him, and his wife who beds a stranger is a presentation of immorality behavior within the ruling class set up.

Karasa who represents the ordinary Zimbabwean is now caught up between a 'hard rock and a hard place', he has been incapacitated, the high authorities have robbed him of his only ox which he uses to plough, which means that without his ox he is not able to fend for his family which questions his existential being as a man who is supposed to be providing for his family. "Those who saw him sitting on the rock talking to himself pointing this way and that way thought he was a mad man", (p.36). Kudyahakudadirwe points out how traumatic situations define people, Karasa now is being defined as a mad person but they do not appreciate the circumstances that have put him through this ordeal.

Kudyahakudadirwe further explores the social trauma scourge in 'Those Shadows on the Wall'. Kudyahakudadirwe uses imagery to suggest that during the periods of crisis children and women are more vulnerable to abuse. The unnamed narrator in the story is a small boy who has since moved to stay with his grandmother together with his mother and his young brother since the arrest of his father.

Kudyahakudadirwe explores the motif of emotional abuse when the narrator, his brother and mother are emotionally abused by the grandmother, the very person who is supposed to protect the children and their mother. Whilst most writers view female victimhood in the lenses of patriarchy, Kudyahakudadirwe takes a different stance on this issue as he exposes the trauma inflicted on women by their counterparts as the mother of the unnamed young narrator suffer emotional abuse in the hands of a fellow woman who is the grandmother of the narrator.

"I can see that Mother is not happy at all. Since we came to stay with Grandmother after father was arrested…."; (p.134). Kudyahakudadirwe also exposes the dysfunctionality of a family unit which comprises the emotional health safety of children who are caught up in such situations. Herbele (1994:31) demonstrates how children in literature offer means of engagement with deeper social phenomena. He further argues that "the significance of child characters derives from the audience's sense of the special nature of children: innocence – which demands protection by and insulation from the harsher aspects of adult society."

Instead, the young narrator and his brother are left vulnerable to emotional and physical abuse, and for the young narrator to feel that they had their freedoms when they were staying at their home. Through the children, Kudyahakudadirwe expresses the psychological harm the children suffer in the hands of family which may leave the children traumatized. The mother of the children is in a dilemma of not able to control the abusive conditions that are subjected to her children as she is also subjected to the same conditions.

Kudyahakudadirwe uses a first-person child's eye narrative view point given by the unnamed child narrator to affirm the position of children when the family fabric is torn. He seems to be echoing Barker's (2011:1) observation of child characters as "exceptional children" whose unfortunate circumstances inform their exceptionality that is their ability to experience and interpret reality differently. According to Nyambi (2016) the combination of first-person narrative viewpoint and child focalization creates a deep sense of intimacy which powerfully persuades readers to align their perceptions with those of the narrator. Kudyahakudadirwe, therefore explores the emotional trauma gaps that are created within family environs. This is evidenced when the narrator says; "Mother looks away. Wells of tears are flooding her eyes, but these cannot be seen on her grotesque shadow dancing on the wall." (p.135). Kudyahakudadirwe uses imagery to depict a deep sense of trauma that is inflicted both on the mother and the child.

4.4 Effects of Migration

Kudyahakudadirwe also depicts trauma *that* is associated with the sudden surge of enthusiasm by most Zimbabweans to go to foreign lands as a solution to the problems ushered in by the Zimbabwean post 2000 economic crisis. According to Pasura (2011), migrant Zimbabwean workers are mainly engaged in unskilled low paying jobs and they also face hostile environments characterized by racism, discrimination and prejudice which probably strengthen their ties with the homeland. This is evidenced by the remittances they send back home. In addition, Zimbabweans in the homeland have high expectations of their relatives in the Diaspora whom they believe are financially secure; Bloch (2008). Taneta, in the story 'A Long Story' is made to believe that across the Limpopo border post there are better life opportunities than the homeland.

Marita is Taneta's cousin who is working in South Africa and she comes home for the Christmas holiday. On Christmas day Marita is dressed to kill sending wrong signals to her friends and relatives that she is better off that side. This is presented by the narrator who describes how Taneta admires her cousin; "She looked adoringly at Marita's Brazilian hair piece and pristine make-up. She only saw such make up in old magazines that the lady teachers at her school used to buy when they had money to spare." (p.17). Kudyahakudadirwe fictionalizes how the issue of elitism is a contributory factor to the Zimbabweans back home who are emotionally put under pressure by their diasporan counterparts. He uses Marita's dressing as a symbol to present an 'elite' life in the Diaspora. The narrator's enhanced image of Marita glorifies the benefits of being in the Diaspora which is assumed it is going to eradicate the poverty in the village life that is presented in Taneta's dressing and her village counterparts.

However, the central point of the story is the depiction of the negative psychological impact of migration on the migrant. Kudyahakudadirwe's depiction of trauma in the Diaspora seems to be supporting McGregor's (2010) sentiments of diasporic displacement that signifies loss of home, social relations, work, rights, predictability and ontological security. Taneta is a representation of diasporic displacement as she has lost basically everything that upholds her ontological security when she gets to South Africa and realizes that she has been duped by her cousin who does not pick her phone calls. "Taneta had never experienced fear of this nature before….All the stories she had heard about crime in South Africa crowded her mind…..She had heard horrific stories of foreigners who had been laced with petrol and burnt alive….at the back of her mind cursed the day she had met Marita at the growth point on that Christmas day";(p.19); this shows Taneta's failure to engage positively with the diasporic experience in her first encounter.

Kudyahakudadirwe's postmodernist style is also significant in his choice of language for his narrative. For instance, Kudyahakudadirwe code switches his narration with a bit of Shona words, for example when the narrator presents the food stocks that are available in a shop that sells food stuff from Zimbabwe that include mufushwa, madora, and derere; (p.23). Another example of syntax oddity is presented when Taneta is expressing herself as a new comer in 'Mzansi' when she says "I only arrived yesterday, mufunge". (p.25) This linguistic creativity significantly contributes to the form of the text as it exposes the trauma thematic issues in the text.

The chronicling of the life of the Zimbabweans inhabitants of the squatter camp where Taneta finally seeks refuge points out to the vulnerability of their existential reality in the foreign land. "After she had used the blue plastic mobile toilet buzzing with green bombers at the edge of the yard, she showed Taneta how to bath in their shack." (p.22).These deplorable living conditions put the diasporans in a precarious position which affects their bodies and psychological state of being. This is evidenced by Taneta who has difficulties in adjusting to the new regime which she is now in. "Taneta was used to another regime of life...." (p.20).

Kudyahakudadirwe also exposes the upsetting of cultural norms and values, this is presented by the narrator on (p.26); "When the offices opened at eight, there was much pushing and pulling for position. Taneta had to put her arms around the man in front of her so that she does not lose her place. All dignity and morality had to be hung on the nail of conscience in such a situation…."; this, therefore, means that Taneta's precarious situation and environment has forced her to compromise her cultural values even if her conscience tells her that it's an anomaly in her culture.

When Taneta finally gets employed as a maid coincidentally, she realizes that Marita, her cousin who has betrayed her, works also as a maid in the same neighborhood. This exposes the disintegration of family life that has been caused by the diasporic pandemic. Although Marita is close family to Taneta she does not live up to her promise that she would help Taneta to settle in the Diaspora. However, in the same context, Kudyahakudadirwe exposes the 'unhu/ubuntu nature of African culture when Taneta gets help from fellow Zimbabweans in the Diaspora who help her to settle and to stand on her own feet.

4.5 Effects of Homosexuality

The culture of homosexuality is not acceptable in most African cultures. It is regarded as an abomination and a decadency of the African cultures. Chibanda (1996) observes that the culture of homosexuality is being imported into Zimbabwe by multinational companies whose mandate is to destabilize the Zimbabwean government. Kudyahakudadirwe explores the theme of homosexuality in the story; 'Loving Beyond Boundaries' exposing the psychological instability on Nyaradzo who has engaged in this taboo social phenomenon. Kudyahakudadirwe is among the few writers who have explored the theme of homosexuality in Zimbabwe.

Postmodernism technique is evident in this story with plot of the story arranged in a harp hazard manner. The story is based on the life in the city that entails inner transformation and constant negotiation of identity between the inborn culture and the physical environment that Nyaradzo is immersed in, so as to forge some sense of belonging to the latter, Nyaradzo experiences psychological and cultural displacement. Nyaradzo and Nyaradzai are twin sisters who are raised single handedly by their mother in a rural set up. Nyaradzo falls in love with one of the teachers at her school, instead of protecting her child the mother supports the relationship because of the material gains they are getting from the young teacher. Nyaradzai gets pregnant with Nyaradzo's boyfriend after the boyfriend mistakenly identifies her as her girlfriend. Kudyahakudadirwe uses the motif of identity in the story to present how loss of identity distorts the psychological state of being of the protagonist Nyaradzai who is forced in a marriage with a man who she never has a relationship with. Keeping Nyaradzo at the same school is unconceivable for the mother, in this state of psychic uncertainty, the mother transfers Nyaradzo to a school in the city. She "feared that what happened to Nyaradzai could also happen to Nyaradzo if she kept attending the same school." (p.44-45). This transition disconnects Nyaradzai from her cultural background, she loses her authentic identity as she adapts to the city life which is a mixed bag of different cultures. However, from a psychoanalytic perspective and in view of her age and vulnerability, Nyaradzo could be perceived as a victim of socio–economic problems that could have left her psychologically wounded.

Kudyahakudadirwe exposes the cultural trauma that Nyaradzo experiences through a letter written by Nyaradzo to her twin sister Nyaradzai chronicling all her experiences in the city life. Nyaradzo describes the city as "where so many strange things can happen, and no one really cares. The people in the city are what I've come to call Halfricans. Because this place is a boiling pot of many cultures, religions and beliefs, people can do what they feel is right for them" (p.46). Nyaradzo seems to be in acknowledgement of the rottenness of the city culture yet she has failed to separate herself from the same as she acknowledges that she has become one of those. The obvious implication of such unstable culturalism is an accompanying sense of insecurity on Nyaradzo who poses a feeling of non-belonging. Therefore, her life in the city is filled with tension which reminds her of "Sodom and Gomorrah"; (p.46).

Nyaradzo feels compelled to engage in a homosexual relationship with Tendai who has been showering her with good life that she has never experienced. Nyaradzo feels "This new life has grabbed me by the throat and threatens to strangle me" (p.48). Many instances in the narrative points out to Nyaradzo's determination to hold on to her past which carries her inborn culture for instance when she passionately recollects her past life in village, which means that she still has an attachment with her roots. This therefore, reveals the psychological trauma that Nyaradzo is going through, she is caught between the hard rock and a hard place, she wants out but at the same time she is trapped in that relationship. The use of juxtaposition in this text clearly shows the psychological torture that Nyaradzo is going through. However, as Kudyahakudadirwe reveals a deeper truth on the culture of homosexuality; it is a bit tricky as well as there is a possibility of deconstructing binaries and challenging reader's beliefs.

Furthermore, Nyaradzo's existential being is compromised, as she lacks identity, she doesn't know who she is as she is also now attracted to Farai the new tenant that they share the house with. She is afraid to let go her feelings towards Farai as she expresses how she fights the temptation to hug him and to do those things she used to do with Gomba her previous boyfriend. She states that; "I'm not sure whether Farai knows that I've a demon that I'm fighting with every day" Besides being traumatized with her self-inflicting problems she has to face the society around her which does not accept this culture. She wants to remain discreet as she fears for her life as presented on (p.51), "Several women have been raped by men saying that that will make them start loving men. Some have even been murdered for being gay or lesbian especially in the townships." She asks her sister to help her make up her mind as she is trapped in between the taboo culture and her ordinary culture.

4.6 Beyond the Post Independence Era

Ngugi (2009:6) states that colonialism has resulted in the "division of the African from his land, body and mind.... Whereas before he was his own subject now, he is subject to another." His statement is an underscore to the importance of re bonding the African pieces together in-order to reclaim the African ontological being. This, therefore, means that Kudyahakudadirwe's text 'Used Condoms' becomes relevant in promoting the search for Zimbabwean authentic identity to those that were involved in the liberation war.

In the story; 'Used Condoms', Kudyahakudadirwe raises some pertinent issues that affect the ontological security of the Mujibhas and Chimbwidos who were "the scouts of the freedom fighters. They did all the dirty work: organizing pungwes, killing sell-outs and burying landmines...." (p.67) yet they don't have anything to show for these scars. According to Fanonian's perception, re-appropriation of land is necessary to substantiate the real freedom; (Fanon 1967). He asserts that land is the most valuable tangible asset that can bring sustenance to the African. The story; 'Used Condoms' makes reference to the post-independence era where part of those that fought the liberation war are going through some ontological disposition as they are trying to figure out their sense of identity in the independent Zimbabwe.

Kudyahakudadirwe in this text uses flash backs to explore the theme of trauma experiences of the Mujibhas and Chimbwidos. The unnamed protagonist who tries to give voice to the traumatic experiences that the Mujibhas and Chimbwidos went through looks back at the thoughts and experiences of his younger version. The story is set on a bus where the unnamed narrator is on a journey to his rural home. The narrator having his bottle of beer, may make a reader anticipate that the narrator would enter the journey space with enough psychological armor to withstand the threats of "unnecessary chattering that would go around me"; (p.66). This clearly shows that the narrator has often unstable psychic moments that he would shut out with beer. In this case the intoxication of beer fails to shut out the 'unnecessary chattering' as he enters into a sensitive psychological realm.

The title of the story may present translation problems to the reader, it may leave the reader with endless connotations that are not coherent with the content of the text. According to Chiridza (2015), titles usually give the reader the clues to content and style of the text as well as providing a frame for the reading of setting and characters. In this case Kudyahakudadirwe takes the title of the story from the quote of the unnamed girl character who refers the Mujibhas and Chimbwidos as being used like condoms. The title therefore, metaphorical gives a representation of how the Mujibhas and Chimbwidos were used in the liberation war only to be discarded after their use as they are not recognized in the post independent Zimbabwe.

It takes back the narrator to the "first Saturday of September 1979;" (p.67) where he relives the events of this particular day back in the liberation struggle. The recollection of events of this particular day by the narrator is triggered by the conversation he overhears between an unnamed boy and girl who are sitting in front of him. He gives a synopsis of the routines of the Mujibhas and the Chimbwidos that they normally did in the liberation war. The narrator being one of the Mujibhas himself, clearly remembers the role they played in the war, and it is clear from the narration that they were a great supporting system to the 'boys'.

According to Kummer (Nd) flash backs are typical symptoms of post–traumatic stress disorder, and their main features are intrusive and vivid images that occur in a waking state. This therefore, reflects how Kudyahakudadirwe explores the psychological entrapment of the Mujibhas and Chimbwidos as the narration is vividly chronicling the events of one particular day in the war as if it is currently happening. Postmodernism characteristics in this text are clearly evident, creating a traumatic text itself. The text questions the reader's psychological comprehensibility of the text, when the reader tries to coherently bring together the concept of 'used condoms', the bus journey and the finer details of the liberation war inorder to come up with meaning. Kudyahakudadirwe reconnects with the reader towards the end of the story when he reveals that that the narrator is still in the bus but it is just his mind that had slipped away.

Be that as it may, Kudyahakudadirwe has exposed the narrator's existential being at the point when his mind becomes conscious again his reaction startles everyone in bus when he realizes that the bus has gone past his dropping off point and everyone thinks he is insane. Taking into account the varying causes of trauma as previous discussed, it is evident that the phenomenon has many roots and may be manifested through a myriad of assumptions. In this text Kudyahakudadirwe depict the phenomenon through the Mujibha's and the Chimbwidos who did not benefit anything from the Zimbabwean government. According to Sachikonye (2003), it's only the war veterans that benefited from the land reform program. Kudyahakudadirwe exposes the experiences of the Mujibhas and the Chimbwidos in the liberation war which proves that the later were supporting pillar to the former hence the traumatic experience for not being recognized for their part they played in the war.

4.7 Summary

Although Kudyahakudadirwe's text is a post-2000, it is evident from the text analysis that he has depicted the theme of trauma from various angles not only picking the post-2000 era but also referring to the colonial era. Kudyahakudadirwe illustrates the vulnerability of the ordinary Zimbabweans who are subjected to different shades of trauma varying from socio political and socio-economic conditions of the post-2000 era. The chapter also looks at how the existential challenges have led the Zimbabweans to migrate to the Diaspora. Kudyahakudadirwe illustrates a new phase of trauma in the Diaspora as their cultural identities are displaced.

Moreover, this chapter has demonstrated cultural discourse of trauma through a story; 'Loving Beyond

Boundaries' whose theme is centered around homosexuality which corrupts Nyaradzo's identity which then has a negative impact on her ontological sense of being. Kudyahakudadirwe also defines trauma in the form of psychic instability in some sects of the Zimbabwean populace who have seen and have been involved in the liberation war in Zimbabwe. It is apparent Kudyahakudadirwe's depiction of trauma is not confined to any particular phenomenon but it goes beyond the wounded heart of a Zimbabwean.

The next chapter provides a conclusion to this study. It gives a summary of the key aspects of the analysis of the two primary texts that have been used in this study as they perceive in the depiction of trauma in the post-2000 fiction writers. Furthermore, the chapter will give an evaluation of the interpretations of these representations. The chapter will finally give a conclusion by offering a suggestion on possible future research that may emanate from this study.

CHAPTER 5

Summary, Conclusions and Recommendations

5.0 Introduction

This chapter focuses on the summary, conclusion, and recommendation of the research study.

5.1 Summary

The scope of this project has been restricted to the depiction of trauma within the selected post-2000 Zimbabwean fiction literary texts with the view of exposing the discourse of the phenomenon in the literary works of relatively new authors. In as much as the motif of trauma has been significantly used in the African literature, not much critical attention has been paid to the literary representations of the phenomenon in Zimbabwean literature. The scholarly representation of the phenomenon is largely centered on established writers that include Marechera, Dangarembga, Vera, Chinodya, Gomo and Chikwava. Yet, this study has proved that trauma is a very common discourse in Zimbabwe's yesteryear and current literary arena. The aim of this study has been to augment the sparse critical scholarship on the trauma trope by demonstrating how it resonates within the set parameters. The analysis of the primary texts and literature review has revealed the different discourse dimensions of the phenomenon that abound the Zimbabwean literature. The study has been made possible by interrogating the fiction of two Zimbabwean post-2000 authors who the researcher deliberately chose to represent the trauma trope in the Zimbabwean context. These are Mwanaka and Kudyahakudadirwe.

This study has provided a backdrop of how the selected authors perceive trauma, this then allows a deeper understanding of the various cultural nuances and perceptions that shape their depictions. The research has been guided by the following key questions; How do the selected texts define and depict trauma? What is the effect of post 2000 Zimbabwean literature on the subject of trauma? And Can Zimbabwean post 2000 literature contribute to change in attitudes towards trauma in Zimbabwe?

The analysis of the two texts has shown how form and stylistic features employed by the two authors reveal the phenomenon at various levels and having various manifestations in the Zimbabwean context. This therefore means that the study provides a conceptualization of trauma as per selected authors' perceptions. The study has defined trauma as evidenced by the writers' depiction of it as culture alienation, identity and as a sign of the socio-political and economic landscapes in Zimbabwe. The texts analysis has demonstrated how the two authors use language, form and style in their narratives to present the phenomenon.

For instance, chapter three of this study has shown that the creative processes that Mwanaka adopts in his text 'Notes from a Modern Chimurenga point to a post–modernist style of writing. The characteristics of fragmentation, disjointedness and non-closure in the sequence of events are deliberately designed to effectively reflect the content of the narrative reflecting all the protagonists' sense of dissociation and fragmentation. The form of the text carries the mental instability that the protagonists suffer as a result of trauma induced by socio–political and economic status of the post-2000 Zimbabwean environment. This study has also revealed that the subject of trauma is mainly presented by using post-modernist writing techniques.

Existential, Psychoanalytic, Precarity and Postmodernism theories and Psychosocial approaches have been crucial in this study as they are relevant in exploring the man's search for wholeness. The theories have given a useful insight into the understanding of the phenomenon based on the various stimuli as evidenced in all the stories from both texts. For example, Chapter four, has exemplified the devastating effects of trauma as the unnamed narrator in the story 'Used Condoms' suffers the psychic scars of the liberation war. This therefore, means that the theories have been significant in highlighting the traumatic experiences of the protagonists in the pre–independence era as well as the post-2000 era presenting the emotional response in the two texts analysis.

Culture and identity fragmentation have helped to explain and clarify various forms of existential precarity that affect the protagonists in both Mwanaka and Kudyahakudadirwe's texts. For example, Chapter four, of the study in the story 'Loving Beyond Boundaries' by Kudyahakudadirwe, the study through existentialism theories has exposed how Nyaradzo is torn within herself as she fails to identify with any of the two cultures that she is caught up in exposing her to ontological insecurity.

The study has also explored gender dynamics at play that expose women as victims of trauma. The researcher being a female herself studying challenging situations that challenge the ontological state of being of a woman has applied feminist psychoanalytical theories in analyzing the literary texts. For example, in the text analysis of Mwanaka's 'Notes from Mai Mujuru's Breast' illustrates how the author tackles the trope of trauma in relation to the borderlines of the female body. Mwanaka uses the explicitly sexual imagery of a woman to explore the theme of corruption that take place in the Chiadzwa Diamond fields resonating with the 'wandering wombs' conceptualization of women. This study has demonstrated that Mwanaka's female protagonists suffer mental repression as they struggle against the socio–economical and socio-political challenges. This is exemplified in Chapter three, in Mwanaka's 'Karidza', where Mrs. Karidza is exposed to psychological trauma as she witnesses her husband being brutally murdered in the act of political violence. Mwanaka's female protagonists have also failed to master their existential reality as they struggle to substantiate their existence and identity in the post-2000 Zimbabwean crisis.

Chapter four has also demonstrated the fragmented gaze that the Chimbwido's and the Mujibhas get when they look at themselves through the colonial mirror. Thus, the process of seeking self-identity and achievement is hampered hence Kudyahakudadirwe's 'Used Condoms' suggest that this act of recollection brings in a dimension of psychological trauma and it takes sane state of being to break the colonial mirror in order for healing to take place.

5.2 Conclusions

The two texts under study Mwanaka's 'Notes from a Modern Chimurenga' and Kudyahakudadirwe's 'The

Big Noise and Other Noises' should therefore be read not only as narratives exposing the authors' traumatic experiences in the post-2000 Zimbabwean crisis but also as texts that provide identity formation. From the texts, the reader is exposed to the knowledge and appreciation of the authors experiences in the prevailing environment. The narrations of the prevailing environment build up the basis of historical account of cultural change in future generations.

Furthermore, the texts under understudy have somehow shown through the technique of characterization and setting both at home and in the Diaspora communities, that people should be able to share the open space that they live bearing in mind of the cultural differences that may exist amongst themselves. Focusing on Agamben's (2000) theorization, of "The people versus people"; the discussion in Chapter 4 in the story 'Between a Rock and a Hard Place'; has explored the chronotopes of class and poverty, demonstrating that the post-2000 crisis naturally stratified people. This means that those that would have been placed in the lower class are vulnerable to psychic problems. This therefore means that the trauma troupe discussion in the entire study points to fact that the psychological being of a person is affected mostly by the people around them.

Recommendations

This study has demonstrated how various shades of trauma are intricately connected to the question of identity. The individuals who are affected by the phenomenon suffer some form of fragmentation and rootlessness in their lives. Zimbabwean society comprises a significant number of people who are in existential crisis instead of finding healing they tend to inflict others as well. In–order to have an ontological secure society, therefore, the researcher makes the following recommendations that there be literary criticism that examines how Zimbabwean fiction represents the psychological healing in the following manner:-

- Resolving the identity crisis
- Knowing the wounds that brought about trauma so that they may be faced and get them healed.

Such an investigation would provide the premise for a valuable research project.

REFERENCES

Primary Sources

Kudyahakudadirwe, C. (2018), Mwanaka Media and Publishing, Chitungwiza, Zimbabwe

Mwanaka, T. R. (2020), Mwanaka Media and Publishing, Chitungwiza, Zimbabwe

Secondary Sources

Achebe, C. (1964), No Longer at Ease, New Yolk: Astor-Honor.

Achebe, C. (1958), Things Fall Apart, Heinemann, London

Achifusi, Ify, G, (1987), The Feminist Novel in Africa, London, Currey.

Agamben, G. (2000), "What is a People", University of Minnesota Press, Minneapolis and London.

Barker, C. (2011), Post-colonial fiction and Disability: Exceptional Children, metaphor and materiality, Palgrave McMillan, Basingstoke.

Butler, J. (2009), Frames of War: When is Life Grievable? New yolk, Verso.

Bhabha, H. K. (1994), In the location of cultures, London, Routledge

Caruth, C. (1995), Trauma: Exploration in memory, Baltimore, MD: Johns Hopkins University Press.

Chidora, T. (2019), Because Sadness is Beautiful?, Mwanaka Media and Publishing, Chitungwiza, Zimbabwe.

Chinodya, S. (1989), Harvest of Thorns, Pearson Education Africa, South Africa.

Chiridza, P. (2015), Zimbabwean Literature II (Fiction) Module AECS 315, Zimbabwe Open University, Harare, Zimbabwe.

Chitando, A. (2011), Narrating Gender and Danger in Selected Zimbabwe Women's Writings on HIV and AIDS, Unpublished Doctoral Thesis, University of South Africa, South Africa

Crawford P, and Baker C, (2009), "Literature and Madness: Fiction for students and professionals" Journal of Medical Humanities, vol 30.

Dangarembga, T. (1988). Nervous Conditions. London: Women's Press

Dangarembga, T. (1993). Neria Film, Media for Development International.

Dangarembga, T. (2006). Book of Not, Ayebia Clarke: Publishing Ltd, Oxfordshire

Eysenck, M.W. (2004). Psychology: An International perspective. Psychology Press 11

Fanon, F. (1967). The Wretched of the Earth. Trans. By Farrington, Constance, Harmondsworth: Penguin

Felman, S. (2003), Writing and Madness, (Literature, Philosophy, Psychoanalysis), Stanford: Stanford University Press.

Foucault, M. (1961), Madness and Civilization, London, Routledge.

Freud, S. (1977), Introductory Lectures on Psychoanalysis, Trans, by Riviere, Joan, London: Allen.

Herbele, M. (1994), The Voice of the Child in Literature, Wayne State University Press, Detroit.

Kahari, G. (1990), The Rise of the Shona Novel: A Study in Development 1890 – 1984, Mambo Press, Gweru.

Kanengoni, A. (1997), Echoing Silences, Baobab books, Harare

Kummer, A. (Nd).https://www.ncbi.nlm.nih.gov>pmc

LaCapra, D. (2001), Writing History, Writing Trauma, Baltimore: Johns Hopkins University Press.

Langa, S. K. (1979), Philosophy in a New Key: A study in the symbolism of Reason, Rite and Art, Harvard University Press, Cambridge.

Marechera, D. (1978), The House of hunger, London, Heinemann

Matibenga, L. (2007), Fighting for Zimbabwean Women, The Guardian, http.www.guardian.co.uk.

McGrath, C. (2010), "Problem of Drawing from Psychiatry for a fiction Writer": Psychiatric Bulletin, vol 26.

McGregor, J. (2010), Displacement of cultural Politics of Survival, Oxford, Berghahn Books.

Mollinger, R. (1981), Psychoanalysis and Literature, Chicago, Nelson Hall.

Muponde, R. and Maodzwa – Taruvinga, M. (2003), Sign and Taboo: Perspectives on the poetic fiction of Yvonne Vera, Oxford, James Currey.

Muponde, R. and Primorac, R. (2005), Versions of Zimbabwe: New Approaches to Literature and Culture, Weaver press, Harare.

Ngara, E. (2009), 'Artists Must Be Responsible Beings' Mazwi a Zimbabwean Journal.

Novikov, V. (1981), Artistic Truths and Dialectics of Creative Work, Trans, by Evgeni, Fillipov, Progress Publishers, Moscow.

Nyambi, O. (2016), Symbolic Childhoods in Zimbabwean short of the crisis, The Journal of commonwealth Literature.

Okolo, M. (2007), African Literature as a Political Philosophy, Zed Books, London.

Pasura, D. M. (2011), Toward a Multisited Ethnography of the Zimbabwean Diaspora in Britain, Identities, 18 (3).

Ramadanovic, P. (2001), "Introduction – Trauma and Crisis: Postmodern Culture" Journal of Interdisciplinary Criticism, vol 11 No 2.

Rieger, B. (1994), Dionysus in Literature: Essays on literary madness, Bowling Green State University, Bowling Green.

Sachikonye, L. (2011), When a State turns on its Citizens: 60 Years of Institutionalized Violence in Zimbabwe, Jacana Media, Sunnyside.

Sachikonye, L. (2012), Zimbabwe's Lost Decade: Politics, development and Society, Weaver Press, Harare.

Saunders, et al (2005), Madness and Creativity in Literature and Culture, Palgrave Macmillan, Hampshire

Shelton, M. D. (1990), Caribbean Women Writers. Massachusetts University Press, Massachusetts.

Somerville, K. (2012), "The Songs of the Maniacs": The four books on madness and creativity, The Missouri Review, Vol 35, No.1

Stone, B. (2004), Starting to Speak: Madness and the narration of Identity, Unpublished Doctoral thesis, University of Sheffield.

Veit-Wild, F. and Chennels, A. (1999), Emerging Perspectives on Dambudzo Marechera. Trenton, World Press, NJ Africa.

Veit-Wild, F. (2006), Writing Madness: Borderlines of the Body in African Literature, Weaver Press, Harare.

Viriri, A. and Mugwini, P. (2009), "Down But Not Out": Critical insights in traditional Shona metaphysics. The Journal of Pan African Studies Vol 2 No 9.

WaThiongo, N. (1982), Decolonizing of the Mind, London, James Currey.

WaThiongo, N. (2009), Something Torn and New: African Renaissance, New Yolk, Basic Civitas Books.

Zhuwarara, R. (2001), Introduction to Zimbabwean Literature In English, College Press, Harare.

Zimunya, M. (1982). Those years of Drought and Hunger, Mambo Press, Gweru.

Mmap Nonfiction and Academic books

If you have enjoyed *Manifestations of trauma in the post-2000 Zimbabwean Literature*, consider these other fine **Nonfiction and Academic books** from *Mwanaka Media and Publishing:*

Cultural Hybridity and Fixity by Andrew Nyongesa
Tintinnabulation of Literary Theory by Andrew Nyongesa
South Africa and United Nations Peacekeeping Offensive Operations by Antonio Garcia
A Case of Love and Hate by Chenjerai Mhondera
A Cat and Mouse Affair by Bruno Shora
The Scholarship Girl by Abigail George
The Gods Sleep Through It All by Wonder Guchu
PHENOMENOLOGY OF DECOLONIZING THE UNIVERSITY: *Essays in the Contemporary Thoughts of Afrikology* by Zvikomborero Kapuya
Africanization and Americanization Anthology Volume 1, Searching for Interracial, Interstitial, Intersectional and Interstates Meeting Spaces, Africa Vs North America by Tendai R Mwanaka
Africa, UK and Ireland: Writing Politics and Knowledge Production Vol 1 by Tendai R Mwanaka

Writing Language, Culture and Development, Africa Vs Asia Vol 1 by Tendai R Mwanaka, Wanjohi wa Makokha and Upal Deb

Zimbolicious: An Anthology of Zimbabwean Literature and Arts, Vol 3 by Tendai Mwanaka

Drawing Without Licence by Tendai R Mwanaka

Writing Grandmothers/ Escribiendo sobre nuestras raíces: Africa Vs Latin America Vol 2 by Tendai R Mwanaka and Felix Rodriguez

Nationalism: (Mis)Understanding Donald Trump's Capitalism, Racism, Global Politics, International Trade and Media Wars, Africa Vs North America Vol 2 by Tendai R Mwanaka

It Is Not About Me: Diaries 2010-2011 by Tendai Rinos Mwanaka

Chitungwiza Mushamukuru: An Anthology from Zimbabwe's Biggest Ghetto Town by Tendai Rinos Mwanaka

The Day and the Dweller: A Study of the Emerald Tablets by Jonathan Thompson

Zimbolicious Anthology Vol 4: An Anthology of Zimbabwean Literature and Arts by Tendai Rinos Mwanaka and Jabulani Mzinyathi

Parks and Recreation by Abigail George

FAMILY LAW AND POLITICS WITH BIOLOGY AND ROYALTY IN AFRICA AND NORTH AMERICA by Peter Ateh-Afec Fossungo

Writing Robotics, Africa Vs Asia, Vol 2 by Tendai Rinos Mwanaka

Zimbolicious Anthology Vol 5: An Anthology of Zimbabwean Literature and Arts by Tendai R. Mwanaka

Love Notes: Everything is Love, An Anthology of Indigenous Languages of Africa and East Europe by Tendai R Mwanaka

Zimbolicious Anthology Vol 6: An Anthology of Zimbabwean Literature and Arts by Tendai R. Mwanaka and Chenjerai Mhondera

BATTLING LANGUAGE RIGHTS GOVERNANCE IN AFRICA: SWISSELGIANISM, UBACKISM, AND THE AMBAZONIA-CAMEROUN WAR by Peter Ateh-Afec Fossungo

Otherness and Pathology: The Fragmented Self and Madness in Contemporary African Fiction by Andrew Nyongesa

Zimbabwe: The Urgency of Now by Tendai Rinos Mwanaka

Zimbabwe: The Blame Game, Recollected essays and Non-fictions by Tendai Rinos Mwanaka

The Trick is to Keep Breathing: Covid 19 Stories From African and North American Writers, Vol 3 by Tendai Rinos Mwanaka

Recentring Mother Earth by Andrew Nyongesa

Zimbabwe: Beyond Robert Mugabe by Tendai Rinos Mwanaka

Language, Thought, Art and Existence: New and Recollected Essays and Non Fictions by Tendai Rinos Mwanaka

Experimental Writing, Africa Vs Latin America Vol 1 by Tendai Rinos Mwanaka and Ricardo Felix Rodriguez

Fixing Earth Anthology: An anthology of Africa, UK and Ireland Writers, Vol 2 by Tendai Rinos Mwanaka

Africa Must Deal with Blats for Its True Decolonisation: Unclothed Truth about Internalised Internal Colonialism by Nkwazi N. Mhango

ROYAL BURIAL AND ENTHRONEMENT IN AMBAZONIA: INTERROGATING THE RELEVANCE OF POSTCOLONIAL EDUCATION IN AFRICA by Peter Ateh-Afec Fossungo

SCHOOL BASED HIV EDUCATION AFFECTING GIRLS IN SELECTED COUNTRIES IN SUB SAHARAN AFRICA by Ivainesu Charmaine Musa

HIV AND AIDS IN ZIMBABWE: A REVIEW ON THE RELATIONSHIP BETWEEN PERCEPTION OF MASCULINITY AMONGST UNMARRIED YOUNG MEN AND THEIR SEXUAL BEHAVIORS by Lucas Kudakwashe Muvhiringi

AFRICA'S CONTEMPORARY FOOD INSECURITY: SELF-INFLICTED WOUNDS THROUGH MODERN VENI VIDI VICI AND LAND GRABBING by Nkwazi Mhango

I Can't Breathe and other Essays by Zvikomborero Kapuya

Ayabacholization Classroom In My Life: The Longest Shortcut To University Education by Peter Ateh-Afec Fossungo

Gathering Evidence by Tendai Rinos Mwanaka

Best New African poets 10th anniversary: Interviews and Reviews by Tendai Rinos Mwanaka

In the footsteps of a Bipolar Life by Ambrose Cato George and Abigail George

Upcoming books

Towards Green Energies: Technologies For Energy Conversion, Storage And The Current Energy Situation In Africa by Blessing Barnet Chiniko

https://facebook.com/MwanakaMediaAndPublishing

www.ingramcontent.com/pod-product-compliance
Lightning Source LLC
Chambersburg PA
CBHW070849160426
43192CB00012B/2365